Cover illustration: 'Scramble' for a Meteor F 8 of No. 77 Squadron.

1. A Republic F-84 Thunderjet of the 27th FEW taking off for a mission in December 1950. The suffix to the 'buzz' number was widely sported by F-84s, due to the main presentation creating many duplicate identities.

WARBIRDS ILLUSTRATED NO. 11

Air War over Korea

JERRY SCUTTS

ARMS AND ARMOUR PRESS
London—Melbourne—Harrisburg, Pa.

Introduction

Warbird 11: Air War over Korea
Published in 1982 by
Arms and Armour Press, Lionel Leventhal Limited,
2-6 Hampstead High Street, London NW3 1QQ;
4-12 Tattersalls Lane, Melbourne, Victoria 3000,
Australia; Cameron and Kelker Streets, PO Box 1831,
Harrisburg, Pennsylvania 17105, USA.

©Lionel Leventhal Limited, 1982
All rights reserved. No part of this publication may be reproduced, stored in a retrieval system, or transmitted in any form by any means electrical, mechanical or otherwise, without first seeking the written permission of the copyright owner.

British Library Cataloguing in Publication Data:
Scutts, Jerry
Air War over Korea–(Warbirds illustrated series; 11)
1. Korean War, 1950–1953–Aerial operations
2. Aeroplanes, Military–History–Pictorial works
I. Title   II. Series
951.9'042   DS920.2.A8
ISBN 0-85368-562-2

Layout by Anthony A. Evans.
Printed in Great Britain by William Clowes, Beccles, Limited.

Often recalled through Harry Truman's words as a 'police action', the Korean War of 1950–53 was a full scale, bloody conflict involving the forces of a dozen nations. That it was more or less confined to Korea was the result of strict United Nations edicts to friendly air forces to avoid overt action into Manchuria and China, although on more than one occasion it appeared that the war would spread to wider conflict. To their credit, UN air forces generally abided by what often seemed to be restrictive political considerations. By late 1950, the air war had been all but won, UN aircraft having overcome the North Korean Air Force and ably supported the drive into the north. Then in November came the mass attack by Chinese forces to rekindle the fighting. The UN command faced a bitter winter of retreat and continual setback that was to last until the spring of 1951.

Along with Chinese ground forces, there appeared the MiG-15, the only fighter able to challenge seriously UN air superiority. High over the inhospitable 'Land of the Morning Calm', the Russian jets began to take a toll of the obsolescent piston-engined aircraft that made up most of the inventory of the Far East Air Force. More serious, the 'first generation' jet fighters were also hard pressed against the MiGs. So it was that the F-86 Sabre, the only Western fighter able to match the MiG, was rushed to Korea.

So successful were the Sabre wings in containing the MiG threat that, in many people's minds, the Korean War is synonymous with that one aircraft. But the air war had many faces and claimed numerous 'firsts' before the armistice on 27 July 1953. These included: the first jet fighter engagements; the initial utilization of helicopters in battle; the first jet operations from carriers; and the development of forward air control techniques. These and other milestones in combat aviation are recorded through the photographs in this book which, although in no way definitive, hopefully will serve to interest historians and model-makers alike.

Jerry Scutts, London 1982

2. Deck activity aboard *Boxer* with arming wires being attached to the bomb load of an F4U Corsair in preparation for a strike, 4 July 1951.

▲3

3. North American F-51 Mustangs were among the first US aircraft to fly combat missions in Korea – and they were still doing so when the war ended. These machines, probably from the 39th Squadron at Ashiya, Japan, are being armed with fragmentation bombs prior to departure for Korea, 6 August 1950.

4. Despite its obsolescence, the Douglas B-26 Invader proved to be one of the most useful types in Far East Air Force's inventory. This example, a B-26C-DT (44-35416), served with the 3rd Bomb Wing.

5. The first Allied nation to respond to the call for assistance in Korea was Australia. Mustangs from the RAAF's No. 77 Squadron were provided which, from 2 July 1950 to 6 April 1951, flew 3,800 sorties before the unit converted to Meteors. Here, two Mustangs are readied for an early sortie.

6. From a single Douglas C-47 used to support No. 77 Squadron, the RAAF's Dakota strength in Korea grew to eight aircraft comprising No. 30 Transport Unit, the badge of which is carried by this example.

▼4

5▲ 6▼

7. HMAS *Sydney* commenced operations in September 1951, having first carried out three months of working up trials around the British coast, during which pilots of Carrier Air Group 21 flew from RN air stations. The group comprised Fairey Firefly AS5s of 817 Sqn., RAN, and Hawker Sea Furies of 805 and 808 Squadrons. Deck handlers fold down a Firefly's wing during the work-up period.

8. Korea was the proving ground for the British Light Fleet Carriers, HMS *Triumph* being the first to launch her aircraft against Communist targets. She is seen here entering Valetta Harbour, Malta, prior to the outbreak of hostilities while Dragonfly HR3 WG719 keeps an eye on the proceedings.

7▼ 8▲

9. One of the most important aircraft of the conflict was the North American Texan ('Mosquito') which, in the hands of pilots of the USAF's 4167th Tactical Air Control Squadron, undertook the hazardous business of directing fighter-bomber strikes. A ground crew are seen here checking over a 'Mosquito' at Taegu, September 1950.

10. Swift servicing was vital if the 'Mosquitoes' were to heed every call to spot and mark targets, often at minimum notice. This crew is 'filling her up' at a typically primitive advance field in September 1950.

11. Lockheed guns. A straight-down-the-barrels view of an F-80, the type that bore the brunt of ground attack operations in the early months of the war.

12. Soon to go into action when this photograph was taken off the California coast, the company of USS *Boxer* cast critical eyes on the technique of this pilot of a Grumman F9F Panther. All Allied carriers became part of Task Force 77 for Korean operations.

13. With a heavy load of mixed ordnance, a Vought F4U-4 Corsair is prepared for a night launch from USS *Sicily*, 16 November 1950.
14. Corporal James Hantelman, an armourer of the 51st Fighter Interceptor Wing, applies a little spit and polish to the nose of a Lockheed F-80C of 25th FBS, December 1950.
15. By 1950, the very heavy bombers of the Second World War had become the mediums of the jet age. Initially pounding North Korean targets in daylight, heavy opposition forced the Boeing B-29 'Superforts' to fly mainly night attacks, for which a black underside was widely applied. Two aircraft of this 98th BG formation are so finished and all machines carry the 'square H' group identity marking, December 1950.
16. RAF participation in Korea was restricted to offshore patrol work and liaison flights over and around the battlefronts. Integrated with US Navy patrols, Short Sunderland Mk Vs of the Far East Flying Boat Wing were in fact under American control. Orders and briefings originated from the ship in the background, USS *Salisbury Sound*, with two Sunderland and two USN Mariner squadrons handling the operations. One of No. 88 Squadron's Mk Vs, RN282, here taxies on the millpond surface of Iwakuni Bay.

▲13 ▼14

15▲ 16▼

▲17 ▼18

19. Mustangs of No. 77 Sqn., RAAF, ticking over on a steel mat hardstanding at Pusan, awaiting the call to take off for the first of two mass attacks by Mustangs of 35th Group. Their target was Chinese positions below the Han River. The Australian unit provided twelve aircraft with napalm, rockets and 'fifty-calibre' armament for the mission on 29 January 1951. Nearest the camera are A68-729 and A68-715.

17. The Mustangs of No. 2 Squadron, South African Air Force, the 'Flying Cheetahs', were committed to the war on 16 November 1950. This former North Dakota Air National Guard F-51D-25 (45-11390) passed through the 6002nd Tactical Support Wing before being assigned to No. 2 Squadron in December 1950.

18. Korea was the first conflict in which helicopters played a significant role. These Bell H-13Ds (Model 47D) carry outrigger stretcher carriers for the evacuation of wounded and are seen in operation in January 1951. The aircraft on the left (51-2446) is the first production D model, that on the right the second (51-2447).

20. The 334th Bomb Squadron seconds away from the bomb release point during a 98th Group mission in January 1951. All aircraft bear the black and yellow diagonal stripes on their tails denoting the squadron and 'tail wind'. The aircraft nearest the camera is 45-21721.

▲21

▲22 ▼23

21. HMS *Theseus* replaced HMS *Triumph* on Korean station on 8 October 1950. Aboard was the Hawker Sea Fury element of CAG 17 (807 Squadron), represented here by FB 11 TF956. Aircraft from *Theseus* recorded the first Sea Fury strikes on Korean targets during the winter of 1950/51.

22. Korean airfield conditions were usually described as 'bad' or 'worse' according to the season. No. 2 Squadron, SAAF, mechanics brave the elements to make ready Mustang No. 312 (44-74432).

23. Sharing the jet ground attack war with Shooting Stars were Republic F-84 Thunderjets, operated by six groups on a rotational basis. Strategic Air Command's (SAC) 27th Fighter Escort Wing flew the first F-84 missions in December 1950, this machine, armed with a single HVAR under each wing, being one of them.

24. An F-51D Mustang of the Republic of Korea Air Force at K-3 Pohang in June 1953. The first combat aircraft the South Koreans had, the Mustang was the subject of an urgent, albeit small, rearmament programme arranged under the 'BOUT 1' programme of 1950. (Picciani Aircraft Slides)

25. To the Marines, the C-119 was known as the R4Q. The -1 version was operated in Korea by the first USMC unit to receive the type, VMR-253. This example, BuAer No. 126735/AD, has typical markings. (Aviation Photo News)

24▲ 25▼

▲26 ▼27

26. A specialized ground attack version of the Corsair, the Vought AU-1 was used exclusively by the Marines. VMA-212's aircraft sported a distinctive arrow-head stripe, as seen here on BuAer No. 133843. Externally, the AU-1 was similar to Second World War Corsairs, as it restored the circular contours of the cowling when the air intakes were relocated. (Aviation Photo News)

27. Korea necessitated the use of some types that had been designed for service in the Second World War but had just missed participation in that conflict. One such aircraft was the Grumman F7F Tigercat, radar-equipped versions of which were used for night interception work in Korea. It was not unusual for some aircraft to have their serial number and unit identification removed, as here on this Marine F7F-3N. (Aviation Photo News)

28. The Fairchild C-119 Flying Boxcar was one of the most important transport types in Korea. Able to lift 15,000lb of freight or 62 troops, the C-119B and C equipped the 314th Troop Carrier Group for the duration of the war. As this example shows, air supply drops were assisted by the removal of the rear fuselage loading doors. This C-119C (49-144) carries typical 314th Group markings.

29. A fully-laden F-51 Mustang of No. 2 Squadron, SAAF, being run-up prior to a mission, probably a little time hence – note that the rocket leads have not yet been 'plugged in'.

30. B-26s of the 452nd Bomb Wing (Light) keep tight formation under the weather during a mission in February 1951. Refurbished for another war, some Invaders retained evidence of their service in 'the big one', including olive drab camouflage. In the foreground is 44-34703, built as an A-26B-DL.

▲31 ▼32

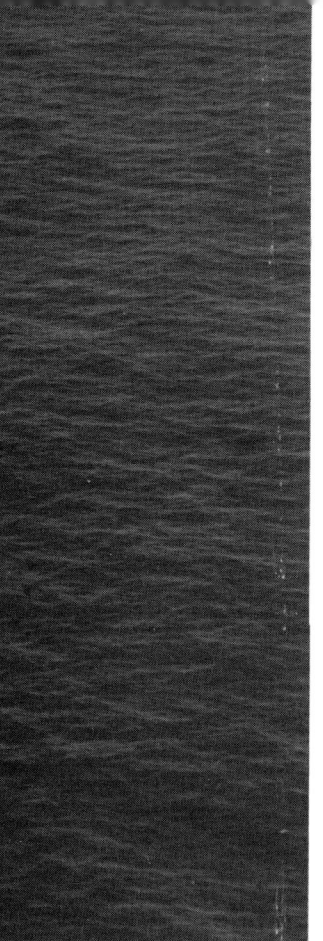

31. HMS *Theseus* finished her Korean operations in April 1951, her air group having flown 3,489 sorties, 2,320 of which were contributed by the Sea Furies of 807 Squadron. Here, one of those sorties is getting underway.

32. Lockheed F-80C Shooting Stars of the 49th Fighter Bomber Wing lined up at an unidentified airfield in the spring of 1951. The nearest machines have the yellow nose and tail trim of the 8th FBS.

33. The then-new H-19 Chickasaw (foreground) joining its older Sikorsky stable-mate, the R-5, in the USAF's 3rd Air Rescue Squadron in Korea, April 1951. Used primarily for rescue, the Air Force's Chickasaws were designated SH-19 and were fitted with a hoist above the door on the starboard side.

34. Heavily laden F-80s occasionally used jet-assisted take-off (JATO) units to get airborne from short runways. The auxiliary rockets are going full blast to lift off this 7th FBS Shooting Star. As well as the long range 'Misawa' drop tanks, the aircraft carries two 500lb bombs.

▲35 ▼36

35. A loading cart weighed down with HVARs soon to be attached to the wing launchers of these Lockheed F-80Cs of the 9th FBS, 49th Wing.
36. A Grumman F9F-2B Panther photographed over Korea on 5 April 1951.
37. To facilitate the rapid turn-round of fighter bombers, the USAF introduced dual servicing points whereby refuelling, checking and minor servicing could be carried out 'on the line'. The system is being used here by 49th FBW on Lockheed F-80s in May 1951.
38. Hooks down, two Fireflies from HMS *Theseus* prepare to land-on. One of the carrier's destroyer screen keeps watch, ready to go to the rescue if any aircraft have to ditch.

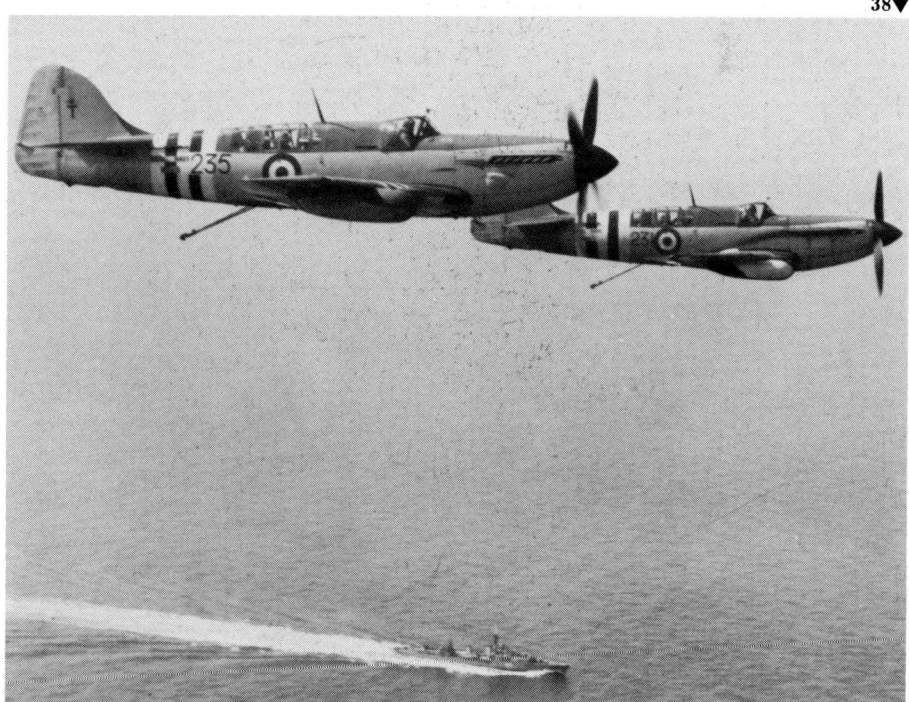

▲39

▲40 ▼41

39. The Vought-Sikorsky Model 327 was called the HO3S by the Marines. Although the Marines had few in number, the aircraft did sterling work, particularly on rescue of the wounded.
40. In the early 1950s, the UN call to arms for Korea was answered by countries willing to provide personnel and equipment. Among those nations was Greece, which contributed Flight 13, Royal Hellenic Air Force, with its Douglas Dakota C-47s. These aircraft operated as part of the 374th Troop Carrier Wing, and their crews were highly regarded by their American colleagues.
41. 'Mosquito' T-6s await the next call as a Combat Cargo Douglas C-47 (315th Air Division) comes in to land, probably at Taegu.
42. One of HMS *Ocean*'s Sea Fury FB 11s getting aloft for an RP-strike.
43. Smoke belching from its rocket assisted take-off gear (RATOG), a Fairey Firefly accelerates down the deck of HMS *Glory* for a fighter-bomber strike.

42▲ 43▼

44. Dumping unburned fuel as they near 'home', a pair of Grumman F9F Panthers prepare to land. The USS *Princeton* (CV-37) has her AA guns trained skywards, just in case. . . .

45. On 26 June 1952, USS *Boxer*'s air group was sent against the rail centre at Hamhung. This Grumman F9F Panther with starburst red nose was flown in that operation by Lieutenant Leonard Gordinier, whose squadron, VF-721, was the first reserve unit to fly Panthers in combat.

46. In June 1951, the Far East Air Force posed this shot of four of its aircraft types tasked with (to quote the original caption) the 'air defence of Japan'. In the event, only the North American F-86 Sabre (below right) was really capable of this duty when the formidable MiG-15 appeared, although the North American F-82 Twin Mustang (top left), Lockheed F-80 (below left) and Lockheed F-94 Starfire (top right) had their successes in aerial combat.

47. In late 1950, FEAF could confidently use former North Korean airfields around the enemy capital, as evidenced by these 18th FBG F-51s being rearmed at Pyongyang.

48. Primed with bombs and rockets, the 18th FBG rolls out for take-off past two unfortunate victims of the hectic pace of operations. In the background, a pair of Douglas C-47s wait for the procession to pass. July 1951.

49. The 'Flying Cheetahs' and the 'Sharkmouths' (12th FBS) pause on the taxiway to allow another Mustang to land.

50. Into the 'morning calm'. An F-51 pilot, who cannot fully appreciate nature's backcloth, tucks up his gear en route for another ground attack.

▲51 ▼52

51. 'Snugglebunny' comes home. After adding 75 missions in Korea to her 65 in the Second World War, B-29 Superfortress 44-69667 was returned to the United States in July 1951 for a major overhaul that was long overdue. In nearly 3,000 hours flying time she had collected numerous holes from flak and was credited with a MiG during her service with the 98th Bombardment Wing.

52. Ancient Korean horse-drawn carts were employed on many forward airstrips to haul infill after the battering from continual jet operations. Here, the workers are 'taking five' around the Lockheed RF-80 dispersals of the 67th TRW.

53. Another important transport type in Korea was the Curtiss C-46 Commando. Commandos were assigned to the 437th Troop Carrier Wing in November 1950 and airlifted supplies from Japan and between bases in Korea.

54. A striking 'tiger tail' marking was used by the F-84 Thunderjets of 49th and 474th Fighter Bomber Wings at different times. In August 1951, black and white tail chevrons identified the 49th.

55. Scratch one Ilyushin. Apart from the MiG-15, the motley collection of Russian aircraft flown by the North Koreans was relatively easy meat for FEAF fighters. This Il-2 paid the price of tangling with a Mustang flown by Lieutenant-Colonel Ralph Saltsman Jr. of the 18th Wing on 20 June 1951.

56. Hoping against hope to get Sabres, No. 77 Squadron, RAAF, received Gloster Meteor F. Mk 8s with mixed feelings in May 1951. The squadron was based at Kimpo when this photograph was taken in September 1951, shortly after which the unit switched from fighter to ground attack duties. The Meteors had proved no match for the MiGs.

▲55 ▼56

57. A Firefly of 812 Squadron piloted by R. Clarke made the 1,000th landing on HMS *Glory* on 4 September 1951. The carrier had only departed from Malta on 19 March that year.

58. Not untypical Korean weather appears to be making the pilot of a Lockheed RF-80 of 67th Wing wonder whether his trip is necessary – but those photographs were always necessary.

57▲ 58▼

▲59

59. Nine Marine transport units (designated HMR squadrons) flew the Sikorsky HRS-1. This example, BuAer No. 127790 of HMR-1, conducts a welcome lift for Marines on 22 November 1951.
60. A neat line of F-51s, believed to be from the 35th Fighter Interceptor Group, October 1951.
61. Jet conversion and combat orientation were carried out on Lockheed T-33 Shooting Stars attached to operational units. This example was one of the strength of the polka-dot marked 45th Tactical Reconnaissance Squadron, which otherwise flew RF-51s and RF-80s in Korea. (Aviation Photo News)
62. The night paint adorning the majority of B-29A-40-BN 44-61623 hides most of its identifying markings, including the 'square H' of the 98th Group across the fin and rudder. The Second World War-originating daylight formation markings were hardly relevant to night operations. (Aviation Photo News)

▼60

61▲ 62▼

▲63 ▼64

65. ▲

63. Various versions of the Douglas AD Skyraider had their combat début in Korea, including the AD-4B, represented here by BuAer No. 132244 from VA-65. From March to September 1952, the unit was part of Air Group 2 aboard USS *Boxer*. (Aviation Photo News)

64. Pictured at K-47 Chin Chan in the summer of 1952 is the F-84E-15 with the 1,000 hours mission marks, also pictured in illustration 75. 'Miss Jacque II' obviously flew at least another couple of hundred hours and in between had the rows of bombs painted out. (Picciani Aircraft Slides)

65. A nice view of a Hawker Sea Fury whose pilot is coping simultaneously with RATOG and the 2,550hp of the aircraft's Bristol Centaurus engine during a take-off from HMS *Glory*.

66. Soon to erupt into a shattering chorus of Merlin and Centaurus engines, *Ocean*'s flight-deck shows the Fireflies and Sea Furies of CAG 20 in mid-1952. In front are Sea Furies WJ238/104, WE725/115 and WJ224/111, all FB 11s. The second Firefly, No. 285 in the left-hand line, has non-standard nose colours and the last two digits of its number on a black panel beneath the spinner. The aircraft next in line lacks the carrier fin code.

66. ▼

▲67 ▼68

67. The US Army's 187th Regimental Combat Team prepare to emplane for the mass paratroop drop on Munsan on 22 March 1951. The largest one-day airborne operation of the war, it involved 135 Fairchild C-119 Boxcars and Curtiss C-46 Commandos. Note the markings on the loading door of the nearest Boxcar.

68. Fairchild C-119 Flying Boxcars head this line of transports, with three C-46 Commandos just visible at the rear. The Flying Boxcars are thought to be from the 62nd TCS, the 'Blue Barons', although two other units, the 50th and 61st, also used the quartered nose device, in red and green respectively. Of additional interest is the Grumman F6F Hellcat (left), the only examples of which to operate in Korea being F6K drones. No. 81 may have been one of the pilotless flying-bomb fighters.

69. Able to take on a variety of 'hard' and 'soft' targets with guns, iron bombs and napalm, this B-26 Invader of the 90th BS, 3rd Bomb Group goes looking for trouble over the grim-looking Korean mountains. A crash in such country could mean months of deprivation for the crew if they survived, with only a slim chance of rescue. Capture by the enemy held its own horrors, unique to the Korean conflict.

70. Nature did all she could to stop mankind waging war in Korea and at best made things very uncomfortable. These 67th Squadron Mustangs are snow-bedecked but not snowbound in the winter of 1952. With the engine hot, the groundcrew will remove most of the snow from the wings by pulling away the tarpaulins which gave some protection to the aircraft's skin.

71. Helicopters were especially appreciated by the ground troops when the weather turned nasty. These 'leathernecks' of the First Marine Division are practising all three main activities of troops in any war, anywhere: sleeping, waiting and actually moving up to do battle. Their transport in this case is a Sikorsky HRS-1, BuAer No.127795.

69▲

70▲ 71▼

72. Marine Sikorsky HRS-1s preparing to lift off from the deck of USS *Sicily* stationed off Inchon harbour.
73. Marines hook up a wire basket of 4.5in rockets for transporting to a forward position; the launcher itself awaits the arrival of a second 'chopper'. Such mobility enabled Marine units to get into position, open fire and leave before enemy artillery could pin point where they had been. Compare the markings on this HRS-1 with those shown in the preceding photograph.

74. High designator numbers were allocated to Navy reserve units, a number of which were called to action in Korea. The two F9F-2s nearest the camera (BuAer Nos 127142 and 127196) represent fighter squadrons VF-831 and VF-837 respectively, while the third aircraft displays no squadron designator.
75. 'Miss Jacque II' was the first Republic F-84 Thunderjet to chalk up 1,000 hours of combat time in Korea – no less than 363 sorties. On the right is First Lieutenant Bruce McMahan, the pilot who flew the 1,000th hour. He is being interviewed with his groundcrew by a Fifth Air Force combat reporter. The markings on 46-2360 tell it all (see illustration 64).

▲76 ▼77

76. The air evacuation of wounded cut combat deaths by 50 per cent in Korea, with the services combining to use fixed-wing transports, helicopters and ships to get the wounded off the battlefields and safely into the hands of doctors and nurses. So proficient was air 'casevac' that hospital ships, initially thought to be essential, were only supplements to the air-lift. This photograph shows an Air Force Sikorsky R-5 with palletized stretchers landing on a hospital ship.
77. Co-operation. Taken at the end of *Glory*'s second war cruise, this photograph shows a USN HO3S-1 (BuAer No. 122714/UP-21) of HU-1 ticking over aft of Royal Navy Dragonfly HR I, believed to be VX595.
78. With some 130 missions already flown, 'Linda Charlotte', the personalized F-84 Thunderjet of the CO of the 49th FBG, was ready for another when this photograph was taken.
79. Early morning during August 1952 sees a flight of 49th FBG Thunderjets en route to Communist targets. The F-84 proved to be the best USAF ground support jet in Korea. This time their target was a Communist supply complex at Namyang-ni near Sukchon, a strike involving over 200 Fifth Air Force aircraft.

78▲ 79▼

▲80 ▼81

80. A Navy fighter pilot climbs aboard his F9F Panther to be launched from USS *Boxer*, January 1952. Along with other painted markings on the Panther's nose is the badge of VF-3 in typically small size. The nose flash is almost certainly red.
81. One of USS *Antietam*'s Air Group 15 Panther squadrons awaits the order to launch during the spring of 1952. The prone 'cat' crew are there to make sure the pilot has his flaps down to generate enough lift after the 'shoot', and a helicopter plane guard watches for any aircraft that fails to launch cleanly.

▲82 ▼83

82. A Bell H-13 Sioux, coded WB-31 on its bubble nose, prepares to take on wounded in a scene straight out of the TV series 'MASH'. Indeed the aircraft is most probably from one of the US Army's Mobile Army Surgical Hospital units.

83. Bomb-laden B-26 Invaders of the 17th Bomb Group heading for a Communist cement plant at Osure on the Haeju peninsula during September 1952. The aircraft trim is believed to be blue, denoting the 34th Squadron.

84. Fragmentation bomb clusters being made up for loading onto the internal racks of the B-26s in the background. Such bombs were very effective against Communist convoys forced to move after dark when FEAF aircraft heavily interdicted the roads by day. The Invaders are believed to have been part of the 17th Bomb Group.

85. Roll 'em out. C-119 Flying Boxcars of the 374th TCG, carrying a regiment of infantry, inch along a taxiway. As well as carrying the troops themselves, the mighty transports also carried their comforts in the form of mail from home, and, in the case of the wounded, literally their life-blood. Cases of plasma were easily accommodated by the C-119s.

▲86

86. Operating with the 483rd Troop Carrier Wing in October 1952, these Boxcars are from the 'Green Hornets', the 61st Troop Carrier Group.

87. A classic shot of two forms of transportation in Korea. Despite the 'obsolescence' of his equipment, the Korean labourer was an integral part of FEAF's air operations when heavy construction vehicles were lacking. The C-119 in the immediate background is probably from the 63rd TCS.

88. A pair of Lockheed F-80s of 8th FBW get airborne for an October 1952 sortie. The yellow sunburst tail markings denote the 80th Squadron.

87▲ 88▼

89. Mission markers appear on both these Grumman F9F Panthers, which were part of Air Group 101 aboard USS *Kearsarge* from September 1952 to February 1953. The Air Group, later redesignated CAG 14, was among the few that had four squadrons embarked flying four different types of aircraft.

90. This unusual shot of a C-46 formation was taken through the window of another Commando as the 315th AD flew another airlift mission in February 1953.

91. Chequer-nosed and plain finished North American T-6 'Mosquitoes' on the flight line at Seoul in October 1952. Each of the more colourful machines is fitted with a pair of underwing panniers.

92. There was not that much rudder area on an F-84 Thunderjet to begin with and the 49th Wings's First Lieutenant John Glina (left) was amazed to find how much more enemy flak had removed during a mission in January 1953. The impact of the shell that did this damage lifted Glina's feet off the rudder pedals, but the aircraft remained controllable.

93. While the fighter bombers fought their war low down, the Sabre wings were keeping the best of the opposition busy thousands of feet above the battle lines. This MiG-15 was one of fourteen downed by Capt. Manuel 'Pete' Fernandez, the 26th ranking Korean jet ace.

94. Among Korea's air combat milestones was the first night 'kill' by a jet aircraft, the Lockheed F-94 Starfire. These Starfires from the 68th F(AW)S represent the unit which scored that 'kill', carrying on the tradition of the squadron's F-82 Twin Mustangs, one of which was credited with the first air-to-air victory in 1950.

▲95 ▼96

54

95. Among the light aircraft types used in Korea was the North American L-17, seen here in US Army markings at a Japanese air base.

96. When the war began, the Republic of Korea Air Force had only a handful of second-line aircraft. That situation was redressed in July 1950 after the ROKAF had had pilots trained to fly Mustangs supplied by FEAF. Instrumental in making the Koreans into effective fighter pilots was Dean Hess, author of *Battle Hymn*. These Mustangs are piloted by members of the ROKAF and are seen shortly before take-off on 18 May 1953.

97. The Douglas C-124 Globemaster added muscle to the Korean airlift. After extensive trials on the airlift by a single Air Proving Ground machine in 1951, the 374th TCW converted two squadrons to the 'big birds'. This example, 51-116, a C-124A, carries the 'Bully Beef Express' badge of the 6th TCS to relieve its otherwise plain finish.

▲98

98. As well as employing the newest types of aircraft, Korea also found work for those that had been serving for years. This Boeing B-17G-80-DL Flying Fortress (44-83411) was used as a transport by Fifth Air Force Headquarters.

99. Several B-26 Invaders were modified with forward-looking radar and an elongated operator's position for use as night path-finders. This example, 44-35867, also has twin .50 calibre machine-gun packs under the wings.

100. 'Superforts' of the 92nd Bomb Group go into action. The big 'mediums' occasionally suffered heavy losses but successfully carried out their mission of destroying most of North Korea's industrial capability.

101. Camera symbols rather than bombs adorn the nose of this RB-29 engaged on photographic reconnaissance missions from Yokota, Japan.

▼99

100▲ 101▼

BEWARE OF BLAST

102. Lieutenant William O'Leary picked up this hole in the fin of his Sabre during a fighter-bomber mission in June 1953. Ground fire caused the damage when the 8th FBW made a diving attack, O'Leary's machine being hit just as he pulled out after releasing his bombs.

103. An F-86F-30 flown by the CO of the 8th FBW at K-13 Suwon in 1953. Decoration, using colours of all squadrons within the wing, was widely applied by commanders, resulting in some very striking Sabres in Korea.

104. Armourers check the firepower of Major William 'Bill' Whisner's 51st Wing F-86 Sabre. Credited with five and a half of the 'kills' marked up here, Whisner's score was sixteen in the Second World War – the kind of experience that made the difference in air-to-air combat in Korea.

105. (overleaf) A good in-flight view of a 336th FIS North American F-86F-1 in the recognition markings carried by all four Sabre wings in Korea.

▲106 ▼107

106. A scene on the flight line at K-9 Pusan catches Invaders of the 34th BS, 17th BW, taxiing onto the pierced steel mat which was essential for air operations from most Korean bases. A-26C 44-34748/Z is nearest.
107. Primed and ready, 'The Golden Bear' of the 17th Bomb Group shares an oil drum revetment with a second A-26C in the summer of 1953. The insignia of 44-34700 may have been inherited from the 452nd Bomb Group, aircraft of which were absorbed by the 17th during the war.
108. 'Rusty', another of the 12th Squadron's shark-mouthed F-51s.
109. A late-production F-51D (45-11538) of the 12th FBS.
110. One of 22 F-86F-30 Sabres used by No. 2 Squadron, SAAF, was No. 601/A (52-4352). Together with the majority of the others, it was returned to the USAF after the war in late 1953.

111. Considering the extent of the ground attack war in Korea, the men who handled the bombs endured a long war under conditions aptly described as 'rugged' most of the time. This armourer is steadying a 500-pounder intended for the Sabre in the background.

112. When the 18th Wing converted to Sabres in February 1953, it continued to fly ground attack missions. This scene, probably taken at K-55 Osan, shows what appears to be a minor 'panic' during a rapid rearm, for the pilot is obviously in a hurry to know what caused a malfunction – maybe a stoppage in one of his guns during the last sortie?

113. A Sabre of 8th Wing receiving its bomb load at Suwon in June 1953. 'The Georgia Peach' carries the nose stripes of a command pilot.

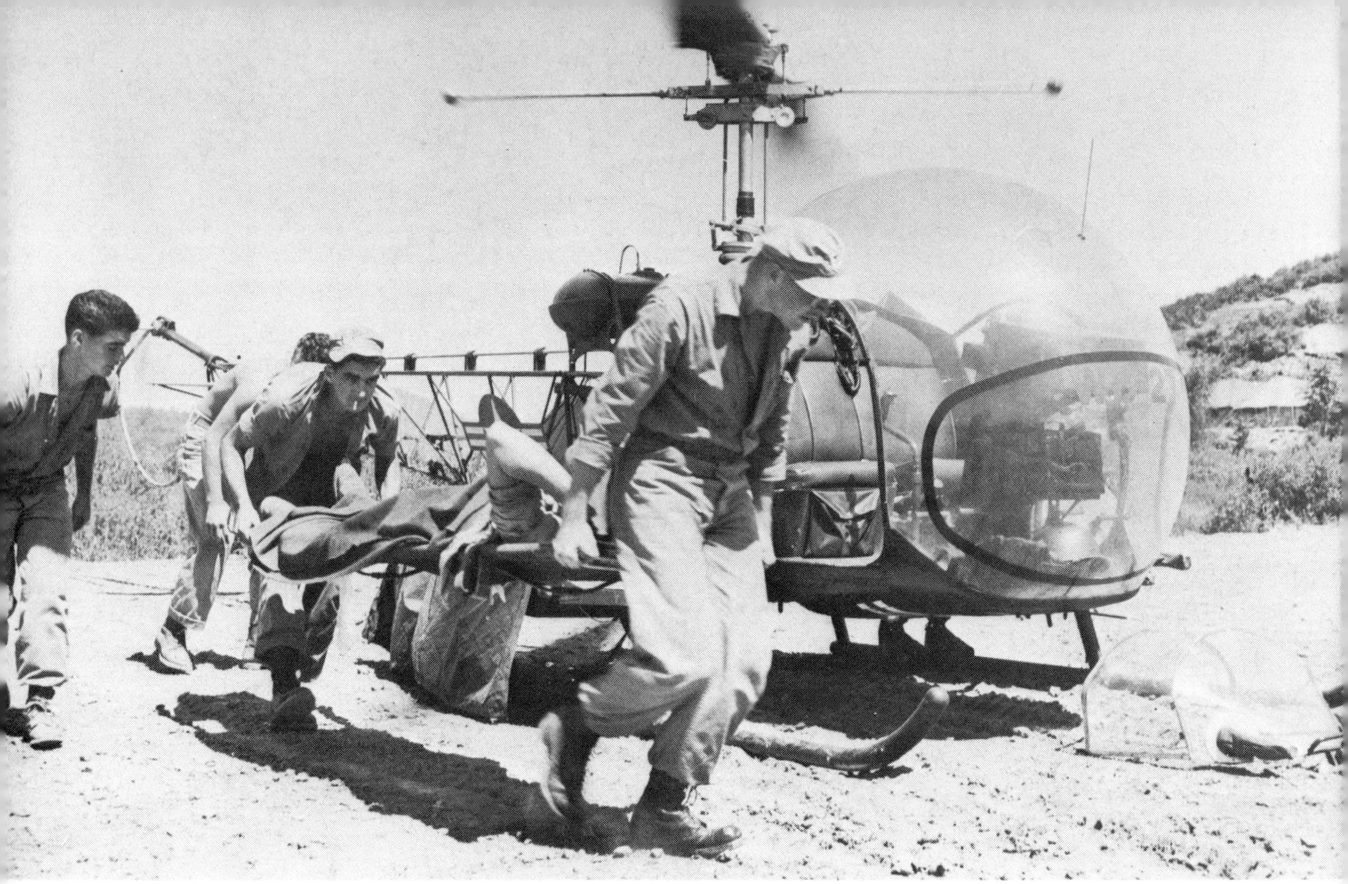

▲114

114. Another urgent call sees one of the Army's MASH units swinging smoothly into action to get the patient into hospital after a flight from the lines. The unmistakable bubble cockpit of the Bell H-13 Sioux gave superb vision over difficult terrain enabling the crew to spot small, often hastily marked out landing areas. This machine carries the coding 'WB-27'.

115. Bringing them back to fight another day did not always apply solely to people. This Sikorsky H-19 Chickasaw has 'hooked' a stripped Cessna L-19 and is whisking it away to a repair depot, where the Birddog will be made to fly again.

116. The strange-sounding name on No. 2 Squadron's 52-4412/G may have been a combination of three names of the pilot's relatives. The Sabre is undergoing a major overhaul in the repair shop at Osan.

117. The enemy close-to. Not until after the end of the war did FEAF get a chance to evaluate a MiG-15, but on 21 September 1953 Lieutenant Kum Sok No landed at Kimpo in MiG-15bis No. 2057, leap-frogging a battle flight of F-86 Sabres on his way down the runway. This photograph shows the MiG at Okinawa, en route to extensive evaluation at Wright Patterson AFB and, subsequently, the Air Force Museum.

▼115

116▲ 117▼

▲118

118. Fleet Aircraft Service Squadrons (FASRON) were established in 1946 and were responsible for the maintenance of all fleet aircraft. They also operated their own machines for various duties. In Korea, FASRON 120's inventory included this Beech SNB-3.

119. Used for liaison and communications duties in the war zone and throughout the Fifth Air Force bases in Japan, the Stinson L-5 Sentinel had been on military duty since 1942. This example, 44-18176, was an L-5E, the version that introduced drooping ailerons operating in conjunction with the flaps.

▼119